THE GREAT
CARD
GAMES
BOOK

Heather Ruth Mackie

For Edwin Rodley and Alexander Higgins

First published by Ashton Scholastic, 1992

This reprint published by Scholastic New Zealand Limited, 1996
Private Bag 94407, Greenmount, Auckland 1730, New Zealand,

Scholastic Australia Pty Limited
PO Box 579, Gosford, NSW 2250, Australia.

Scholastic Inc
565 Broadway, New York, NY 10012-3999, USA.

Scholastic Canada Ltd
123 Newkirk Road, Richmond Hill, Ontario L4C 3G5, Canada.

Scholastic Limited
1–19 New Oxford Street, London, WC1A 1NU, England.

9 8 7 6 5 4 3 2   6 7 8 9 / 9

Printed in Malaysia, by SRM Production Services
Designed and Illustrated by Paul Woodruffe

THE GREAT CARD GAMES BOOK

Heather Ruth Mackie

Scholastic

Auckland Sydney New York Toronto London

Contents

A Note from the Author

It's fun to play card games on wet days or during the holidays, and there are already many different well-known games to play.

The aim of this book is to provide you with even more ideas for using a pack of cards. Not only are there some entirely new games, but I have also given suggestions for laying out the card pack in various ways and using it as though it were a board game. You roll a dice, just like in a conventional board game, and move playing tokens along the line of cards.

After playing the games in this book, I'm sure you'll think up more ideas of your own using a pack of cards.

Happy playing!

Heather Ruth Mackie

Introduction

Making Your Own Card Pack

All the games in this book use ordinary playing cards. For some games you will need two packs. If you do not have a pack of cards, you can make your own as follows:

1. Cut thin cardboard into fifty-four pieces measuring 6 cm x 4 cm.
2. Using felt-tipped or ballpoint pen, mark each card with a suit (Hearts, Diamonds, Clubs, Spades) and a number until you have a complete set (13 cards) of each suit: Ace, 2, 3, 4, 5, 6, 7, 8, 9, 10, Jack, Queen, King. The two remaining cards are the Jokers.

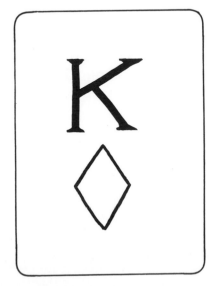

3. In the top left-hand corner, and in the bottom right-hand corner (but upside down), mark each card as follows:

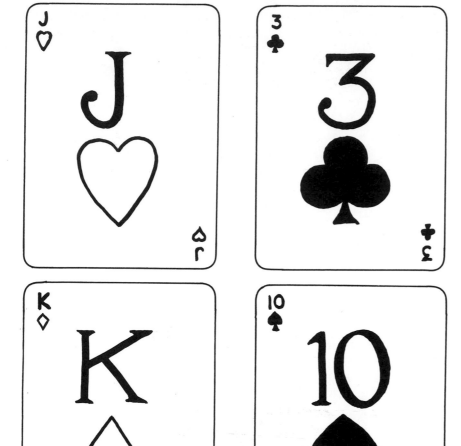

This will make each card easily identifiable when held fan-like in the hand.

4. The two Jokers do not belong to any suit and are not needed for every game. Jokers are sometimes used in games as substitutes for other cards to enable a player to win more easily. They can also win extra points in some games.

Royal Face Cards

This is the term used for the Jack, Queen and King. Their faces are shown on all four suits (Hearts, Diamonds, Clubs and Spades).

Cutting the Deck

To cut the deck one person takes a pile of cards from the top of a face-down pack with one hand, turning them over to reveal a card.

Who Starts?

Shuffle the cards and place pack face down. Each player in turn cuts the deck. Counting a Jack to be worth 11, a Queen to be worth 12, a King to be worth 13, and a Joker to be worth 14, the player showing the card with the highest number has the first turn.

Players sit in a circle and play in a clockwise direction. If there are only two players, they sit opposite each other.

A Variety of Games

Time Me!

Materials Required:

one pack of cards, with Jokers removed
watch or clock that measures minutes and seconds
paper and pencil

Before You Start:

1. Make scoresheet by heading paper with players' names, as shown:

Tim	Bess	Bob	April
2·55 to			

2. A timekeeper is chosen to record players' times.

Aim of the Game: To collect the full set of one suit in the shortest possible time

Number of Players: Three or more

How to Play:

1. Decide who will go first. This player sits facing the others who sit in a semicircle.
2. He/she shuffles the pack and deals all the cards to the other players. (It doesn't matter if cards are dealt unevenly.)
3. The first player decides which suit to collect and the timekeeper makes a note of the time beneath his/her name. The player then asks each person in turn for a card of that suit.
4. Player whose turn it is continues asking until he/she has the whole suit from Ace to King. Timekeeper writes down finishing time.
5. Record each player's time in this way until every player has had a turn.
6. The player who takes the shortest time to collect a full set of his/her chosen suit is the winner.

Variation: Beat the Clock!

Before You Start:

1. On paper, write down the winning time from the first game.
2. Underneath write players' names as before.
3. Use the clock or watch again.

How to Play:

1. Play as before, only now players aim to beat the shortest time.
2. Record the times taken by players, as before.
3. The player who has beaten the shortest time is the winner. If two or more players manage to do this, the winner is the player who has the *new* shortest time.

Run for It!

Materials Required:

one pack of cards, with Jokers removed

Aim of the Game: To collect a complete suit

Number of Players: Two, three or four

How to Play:

1. Players each choose a suit to collect — Hearts, Clubs, Diamonds or Spades.
2. Shuffle card pack and lay cards out in a haphazard fashion, face down.
3. Decide who will go first.
4. Each player picks up one card.
5. First player starts by asking any other player for a card of the suit he/she is collecting. For example, if player is collecting Clubs he/she may ask for the 8 of Clubs. Card must be surrendered by other player if held.
6. Player continues asking for cards he/she needs until denied, when turn is over.
7. At the start of each player's turn, EVERY player picks up a card.
8. As players receive their cards, according to the suit they have chosen, they place the cards face up in front of them.

9. The first player to collect a complete suit is the winner.

   Note: If game has only two or three players and someone picks up a card from a suit that is not being collected, that card is discarded and player's turn is over.

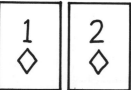 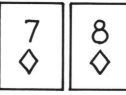

Steal

Materials Required:

one pack of cards, with Jokers removed

Aim of the Game: To be the first player to run out of cards

Number of Players: Any number

How to Play:

1. Shuffle card pack.
2. Decide who will go first.
3. Cards are dealt, five to each player, by the player on the right of the person who starts. Players must not see each other's cards. The pack is then placed face down and the top card turned over to form the Discard Pile.
4. From the cards held in their hands, players aim to form runs of three cards or more of the same suit as illustrated:

5. The player whose turn it is can choose to either:
   a) pick up the top card from the pack
   b) pick up a card from the Discard Pile
   c) 'steal' a card from another player's hand without looking to see what it is
6. Player then checks the six cards he/she holds to see if a run of at least three cards can be made. If so, cards are placed face up in front of him/her. Player then chooses a card to discard and places it on the Discard Pile. Turn is now over.
7. If player does not have a run, he/she still discards one card as above.
8. During their turn, players can add to other players' runs if they wish. This helps them to run out of cards sooner.
9. If the game is not over but the pack is finished, turn over the Discard Pile and continue playing from that.
10. The first player to run out of cards is the winner.

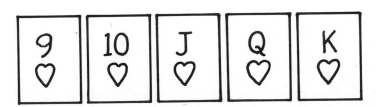

Scatter

Materials Required:

one pack of cards
paper and pencils (for scoring)

Before You Start:

1. Place the Key where players can refer to it easily. (You may copy it onto a separate piece of paper if you wish.)

Key

If you turn over a:	Write down these letters:
Joker	a e i o u
King	a j h n
Queen	q g r p
Jack	i b u f
10	m e n s
9	w h c m
8	o v k d
7	d i t w
6	l e v a
5	o l t x
4	f s c z
3	p j y u
2	x b g y
1	r z a k

2. Supply players with paper and pencils for recording letters.

Aim of the Game: To be the first player to make a word of five or more letters

Number of Players: Two or three

How to Play:

1. Shuffle card pack and scatter cards face down on playing area.
2. Decide who will go first.
3. Each player in turn lifts up one card and, referring to the Key, writes down the appropriate letters on his/her paper. Player leaves card upturned. It is not used again and turn is over.
4. Game is over when there are not enough cards left to complete a round. (There may be some cards left unturned.)
5. Players now attempt to make a word of five or more letters from the letters they have written down.
6. The first player to make a word calls out SCATTER WORD! and is the winner.

7	d i t w
4	f s c z
10	m e n s
K	a j h n

tennis

Groups

Materials Required:

one pack of cards

Aim of the Game: To be the first player to run out of cards

Number of Players: Any number

How to Play:

1. Shuffle card pack.
2. Decide who will go first.
3. The player sitting on the right of the player who starts deals out the cards evenly. Any leftover cards are placed face up in centre of playing area. This is the Discard Pile.
4. Players form a pack with their cards, keeping them face down.
5. Players lift the top five cards from their packs and try to make a set of three or more cards, all of the same number but belonging to any suit. Jokers can be counted as any card to make a set. For example, if a player has two 4s and a Joker, this makes a set of three 4s. These cards are then placed face up:

6. The player who starts first picks up one more card from his/her card pack (six cards now held). Or, if player prefers, he/she can pick up the entire Discard Pile. If player can make a set of three or more, these cards are placed face down in front of him/her.
7. After player has made a set, he/she chooses one card to discard and this is placed face up in centre of playing area. Turn is now over.
8. During their turn, players can add to other players' sets with appropriate cards if they wish. This helps them to run out of cards sooner.
9. The first player to run out of cards is the winner.

Pick Up

Materials Required:

one pack of cards

Aim of the Game: To be the first player to collect five cards of the chosen suit

Number of Players: Two, three or four

How to Play:

1. Shuffle card pack. Lay cards out in a haphazard fashion, face down.
2. Decide who will go first.
3. Each player chooses a suit which must be different from the other players.
4. Players take turns picking up one card at a time. If this card is of the chosen suit, player keeps it and places it face up in front of him/her. If not, player replaces it. *(Do not let other players see the card!)*
5. The first player to collect five cards of his/her chosen suit is the winner.

Variation:

1. Any number of players may play, with each person choosing a different number or Royal Face card.
2. The first player to collect three cards of that number or Royal Face is the winner.

Sevens

Materials Required:

one pack of cards, with Jokers removed

Aim of the Game: To be the first player to run out of cards

Number of Players: Any number

How to Play:

1. Shuffle card pack.
2. Decide who will go first.
3. The player sitting on the right of the player who starts deals seven cards to each player. Remaining cards are placed face down.
4. Players check for a 7 in their cards.
5. The player who starts puts down any 7 he/she holds, plus any other cards of the same suit (6, 5, etc.) so long as the cards run in numerical order either up or down. If the player doesn't have a 7, he/she picks up top card from pack. If a 7 is picked up the player may place it down, along with consecutive cards of the same suit if he/she has them.

6. Turn is over when a player has put down all the cards he/she can. Next player may add to existing run(s) and/or begin a new run with a 7.
7. If a player runs out of cards, he/she picks up the top card from the pack and starts again.
8. Once the pack has run out, the first player to use up his/her cards by placing them appropriately is the winner.

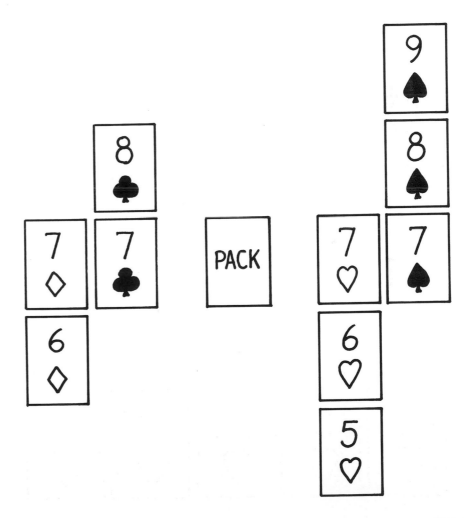

Memory

Materials Required:

two packs of cards

Aim of the Game: To collect the most pairs of cards

Number of Players: Any number

How to Play:

1. Shuffle card packs together and lay out face down in the shape of a rectangle.
2. Decide who will go first.
3. Players lift two cards at each turn. If cards match exactly (i.e. two 5s of Hearts, two Queens of Clubs), player keeps the pair of cards.
4. Cards which do not match are replaced face down and turn is over.
5. The player who has the most pairs when all the cards have been used is the winner.

   Note: It helps to remember what cards are turned over during the game and where they are.

Greed!

Materials Required:

one pack of cards, with Jokers and Royal Face cards
   removed
a coin to toss

Aim of the Game: To be the first player to hold as
                                    many 8s, 9s and 10s as possible

Number of Players: Three

How to Play:

1. Decide by tossing the coin who will be Jack, who will
   be Queen and who will be King.
2. Shuffle card pack.
3. Decide who will go first.
4. The player sitting on the right of the player who starts
   deals the cards. The one card left over is placed face
   up to start the Discard Pile.
5. Players aim to get the highest cards (8s, 9s and 10s).
   Each player in turn asks any other player: 'Jack/
   Queen/King, do you have a Spade?' If a Spade is
   held it must be surrendered, but player who is asked
   attempts to give a Spade of the lowest possible
   number.
6. If the suit requested is not held, turn is over. If the suit
   requested is surrendered, player whose turn it is may
   keep asking until denied.
7. Each player must discard one card after his/her turn is
   completed, choosing the lowest possible number. As
   game progresses, players will hold more and more
   cards with high numbers, and less cards with low
   numbers.
8. When a player holds nothing but 8s, 9s and 10s
   he/she drops out but retains cards. As soon as all
   players hold only 8s, 9s and 10s, everyone lays down
   their cards, face up.
9. The player with the most 8s, 9s and 10s is the winner.

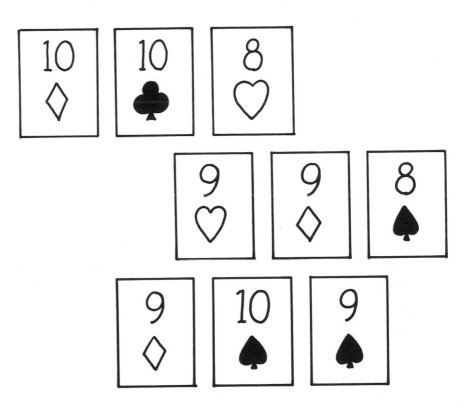

Games Using Counters

Flip

Materials Required:

one pack of cards
2 counters (one to flip the other)
paper and pencils (for scoring)

Before You Start:

Supply paper and pencils for players to record scores.

Aim of the Game: To score the most points

Number of Players: Any number

How to Play:

1. Shuffle card pack and lay out face up in the shape of a rectangle (nine cards across, and six down).
2. Decide who will go first.
3. Players use one counter to flip the other onto the cards, tiddlywinks fashion, aiming for the highest-scoring cards.
4. When counter lands on the numbered cards, player scores that number of points. For Royal Face cards, scores are as follows:

JACK 15
QUEEN 20
KING 25
JOKER 30

5. The first player to reach 100 points is the winner.

Variation:

Small sweets are placed on cards. Players take turns to flip a counter and if it lands on a card holding sweets, they may choose one. The game is over when all the sweets have gone.

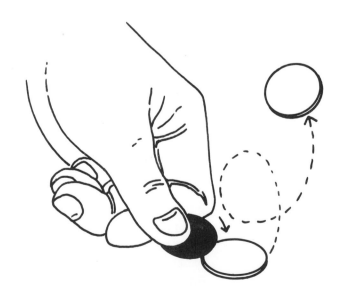

Badges

Materials Required:

one pack of cards
paper and pencils (for scoring)
thin cardboard, approximately 20 cm x 20 cm
extra cardboard, for Badges
scissors
felt-tipped or ballpoint pen
3 small safety pins
sticky tape
plastic cup (for drawing circles)
coloured pencils (optional)
2 counters (one to flip the other)
playing tokens
timer

Before You Start:

1. Using the extra cardboard, make Badges by drawing circles around the cup and cutting out.
2. In pen, write Jack, Queen or King on each. Fasten a safety pin on the pack of each with tape, as shown:

front

back

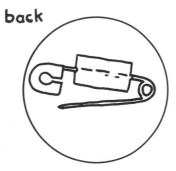

3. On the 20 cm x 20 cm piece of cardboard, make a Numbered Card by drawing lines from corner A to corner B, and from corner C to corner D. Where they cross in the centre, place the plastic cup and draw a circle. Write figures on the Numbered Card, as shown:

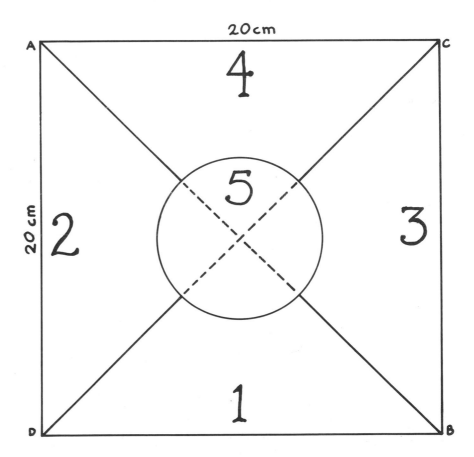

4. If you wish, colour in Badges and Numbered Card with coloured pencils.

5. Supply players with paper and pencils for scoring.

Aim of the Game: To score the highest number of points in the time allowed

Number of Players: Three

How to Play:

1. Place counters for flipping beside Numbered Card.
2. Shuffle card pack and lay out face up in a circle. Decide which card is START and place all tokens on this. Or, use the Joker as the START card and place all tokens on this.
3. Decide who will go first.
4. Player whose turn it is flips one counter with the other, tiddlywinks fashion, so that the flipped counter lands on a number on the Numbered Card. He/she then moves his/her token that number of cards around the circle, until the token stops on a card.
5. Player scores the number of points shown by the number on the card. For Royal Face cards, scores are as follows:

**If you land on a JACK score 15 points
But if you *are* the Jack and you land on a Jack, score 30 points**

**If you land on a QUEEN score 15 points
But if you *are* the Queen and you land on a Queen, score 30 points**

**If you land on a KING score 15 points
But if you *are* the King and you land on a King, score 30 points**

If you land on the JOKER score 20 points

6. Set the timer for 10 or 15 minutes, depending on how long you want to play. When the bell rings, game is over and players total their scores.
7. The player with the highest score is the winner.

Variation:

1. Shuffle card pack and lay cards face up in a long line which can be straight or curved. Decide which end is START and which is FINISH.
2. Players move tokens and score as described above. When all tokens have crossed FINISH, scores are totalled.
3. The player with the highest score is the winner.

Games Using Playing Tokens

Family Circle

Materials Required:

one pack of cards
playing tokens
dice and shaker
paper and pencils (for scoring)

Before You Start:

1. Supply players with paper and pencils for scoring.
2. Each player chooses a suit and writes this on his/her paper as follows:

Aim of the Game: To be the first to land on the King, Queen and three numbered cards of a chosen suit

Number of Players: Any number

How to Play:

1. Shuffle card pack and lay out face up in a circle. The Joker is the START card.
2. Decide who will go first.
3. All tokens are placed on the Joker.
4. Players roll dice and move tokens around circle in a clockwise direction. Players must land on the King (father), Queen (mother), and three numbered cards of their chosen suit, recording these landings as follows:

5. Players landing on cards not of their chosen suit have nothing to record and turn is over.
6. The first player to score a whole family is the winner.

Pairs

Materials Required:

one pack of cards
thin cardboard
scissors
felt-tipped or ballpoint pen
red and black marking pens or coloured pencils
paper and pencils (for scoring)
playing tokens
dice and shaker

Before You Start:

1. Make a Red Card Pack and a Black Card Pack by cutting the cardboard into 7 cm x 4 cm rectangles. Make as many as you like, as long as there are at least twelve of each. It's not necessary to have the same number of Red and Black Cards.
2. Use the red pen to mark the backs of the Red Card Pack and the black pen for the Black Card Pack, making a pattern of your choice. For example:

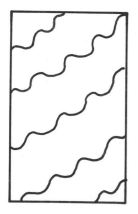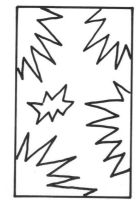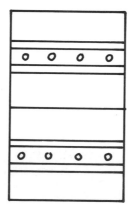

3. In pen, write one tongue twister on the front of each card in the Red Card Pack. Here are some suggestions but you can make up more of your own if you want a bigger pack.

A noisy noise annoys an oyster
Baby Belinda blows big bubbles
Cheeky Charlie chews chocolate cheerfully
Russell Rabbit runs round radishes
Peter Piper picked a peck of pickled peppers
Round the rugged rocks the ragged rascals ran
I'm not a thistle sifter, I'm the thistle sifter's son
Andy and Aggie ache all over
Sally sells seashells on the seashore
Happy Horace hopes he has a hippopotamus
Donald Duck downs a delicious drink
Merry Melissa makes a muddy mess

4. In pen, write one set of pairing words on the front of each card in the Black Card Pack. Here are some suggestions:

arms/legs	boy/girl	man/lady
egg/eggcup	cup/saucer	table/chair
snakes/ladders	pen/pencil	knife/fork
spoon/fork	brush/comb	hat/coat
brush/shovel	scarf/gloves	shoes/socks

5. Supply paper and pencils to players for scoring.

Aim of the Game: To score the most points

Number of Players: Any number

How to Play:

1. Shuffle both Red and Black Card Packs separately and place face down.
2. Shuffle card pack and lay out face up in a long line as shown. This line can be straight or curved. Decide which end is START and which end is FINISH.

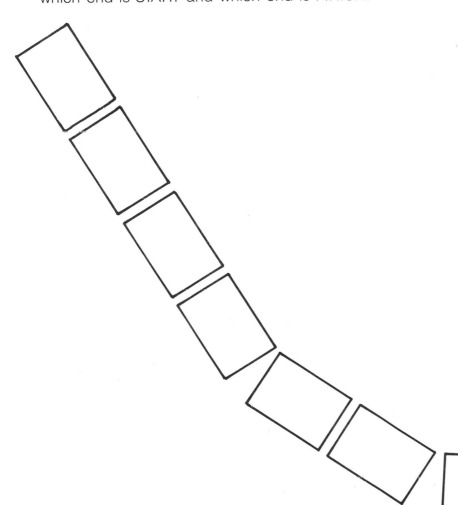

3. Decide who will go first.
4. As players roll the dice and move tokens according to the number shown, the token will land on either a red or black card. For Royal Face cards, scores are as follows:

JACK 15
QUEEN 20
KING 25

5. If player lands on a red card, he/she lifts the top card from the Red Card Pack and reads the tongue twister five times. If player is able to read it successfully, he/she scores the number of points indicated by the card on which token has landed.
6. If player lands on a black card, the player OPPOSITE lifts the top card from the Black Card Pack and reads out the first word. The player whose turn it is must come up with the matching word. If correct, player scores the number of points indicated by the card on which token has landed. If not, no points are scored and turn is over.
7. Game is over when all the tokens have crossed FINISH. Scores are totalled and the player with the highest score is the winner.

Directions

Materials Required:

one pack of cards, with Jokers and two Aces removed
playing tokens
felt-tipped or ballpoint pen
thin cardboard
scissors
paper and pencils (for scoring)

Before You Start:

1. Cut cardboard into 7 cm x 4 cm rectangles to make Direction Card Pack.
2. In pen, write Directions on these cards as follows:

   2 up, 2 right   3 down, 1 left
   1 right, 2 down   2 left, 1 down
   3 up, 2 left   1 left, 3 right

   Make up more Directions of your own, and then duplicate them so you have two cards for each Direction. Form into a pack.
3. Supply players with paper and pencils for scoring.

Aim of the Game: To be the first player to reach 50 points

Number of Players: Any number

How to Play:

1. Shuffle Direction Card Pack and place face down.
2. Shuffle card pack and lay out face up in the shape of a rectangle (ten cards across and five down).
3. Decide who will go first.
4. Players place tokens on any card they choose.

5. Player who starts lifts the top card from the Direction Card Pack and moves his/her token according to the instruction, then returns card to the bottom of the pack.
6. If a Direction leads a playing token off the edge of the card rectangle, token should be stopped and remaining part of Direction completed.
7. Players score points according to the card on which their tokens land after following and completing each Direction. For Royal Face cards, scores are as follows:

   JACK 15
   QUEEN 20
   KING 25

8. The first player whose score totals 50 is the winner.

   Note: Two or more card packs could be used for this game, making a bigger rectangle.

Variations:

1. Instead of aiming for a winning score of 50, use a timer and set it for 10 minutes. The player with the highest score when the bell rings is the winner.

   OR

2. Make a lot more Direction Cards so the game lasts longer. Do not return Direction Cards to bottom of pack after use but put them aside. When Direction Card Pack is finished, game is over. The player with the highest score is the winner.

   OR

3. Players take turns to read out Directions. All players move their tokens accordingly at the same time, recording scores as they go. Use this method for any of the games.

   OR

4. Instead of aiming for the highest score, players aim for the lowest, and player with the lowest total wins.

Same Suit

Materials Required:

one pack of cards, with Jokers removed
playing tokens
dice and shaker
paper and pencils (for scoring)

Before You Start:

1. Each player chooses a suit and writes this on his/her paper. More than one player may choose the same suit.

Aim of the Game:
To be the first player to land on five cards of the chosen suit

Number of Players:
Any number

How to Play:

1. Shuffle card pack and place cards face up in a circle.
2. Each player places token on any card *not* of his/her suit.
3. Decide who will go first.
4. Player rolls dice and moves token around circle in a clockwise direction. If token lands on a card of the chosen suit, player places a tick on his/her paper and rolls the dice again. If token does not land on a card of the chosen suit, turn is over.
5. The first player to collect five ticks is the winner.

Variation:

1. Instead of collecting ticks, players score according to the number shown on the card. For Royal Face cards, scores are as follows:

   KING **25**
   QUEEN **20**
   JACK **15**

2. Game is over when all players have landed on five cards of their chosen suit. Scores are totalled and player with the highest score is the winner.

Times What?

Materials Required:

one pack of cards, with Royal Face cards and Jokers
  removed
paper and pencils (for scoring)
thin cardboard
scissors
felt-tipped or ballpoint pen
playing tokens
calculator (optional)

Before You Start:

1. Cut cardboard into 3 cm x 3 cm squares for
   Numbered Card Pack.
2. In pen, write one number from 1 to 10 on each card.
   Make as many sets of 10 as you wish.

3. Supply players with paper and pencils for scoring.

Aim of the Game: To earn the highest number of points

Number of Players: Any number

How to Play:

1. Shuffle the Numbered Card Pack and place face
   down.

2. Shuffle the card pack and lay out face up in a long
   line which can be straight or curved. Decide which
   end is START and which end is FINISH.
3. Decide who will go first.
4. Player starts by lifting the top card of the Numbered
   Card Pack and laying this card face up. Player then
   moves his/her token along the line of cards according
   to the number shown on the Numbered Card.
5. When player's token stops at a card, player multiplies
   the number on it by the number on the Numbered
   Card. The answer can be checked by another player
   using the Multiplication Table provided, or a calculator
   if available.
6. If answer is correct, player scores that number of
   points and records them on his/her paper.
7. When turn is over, the Numbered Card is placed at
   the bottom of the Numbered Card Pack.
8. When all playing tokens have crossed FINISH, game
   is over.
9. The player with the highest score is the winner.

Multiplication Table

	1	2	3	4	5	6	7	8	9	10
1	1	2	3	4	5	6	7	8	9	10
2	2	4	6	8	10	12	14	16	18	20
3	3	6	9	12	15	18	21	24	27	30
4	4	8	12	16	20	24	28	32	36	40
5	5	10	15	20	25	30	35	40	45	50
6	6	12	18	24	30	36	42	48	54	60
7	7	14	21	28	35	42	49	56	63	70
8	8	16	24	32	40	48	56	64	72	80
9	9	18	27	36	45	54	63	72	81	90
10	10	20	30	40	50	60	70	80	90	100

Reds or Blacks

Materials Required:

one pack of cards
playing tokens
dice and shaker
paper and pencils (for scoring)

Before You Start:

1. Supply players with paper and pencils for recording ticks.
2. Each player decides whether to be Black or Red and heads up his/her paper as follows:

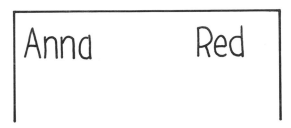

Aim of the Game: To land on the most black or red cards

Number of Players: Any number

How to Play:

1. Shuffle card pack and lay cards face up in a line which can be straight or curved. Decide which end is START and which is FINISH.
2. Decide who will go first.
3. Players roll dice and move tokens along line of cards. If token lands on a black card and player has chosen Black, he/she ticks paper and turn is over.

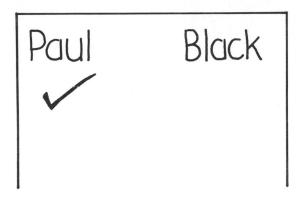

4. If token lands on Royal Face Cards, play is as follows:

   Any colour KING: go back two cards
   Any colour QUEEN: go forward two cards
   (If tokens moving backwards or forwards land on another King or Queen, player remains on that King or Queen and turn is over.)
   A JACK of your chosen colour: score 2 ticks
   JOKER: score 5 ticks

5. When all players' tokens have crossed FINISH, game is over. The player with the highest number of ticks is the winner.

Snakes and Ladders

Materials Required:

two packs of cards, with Jokers removed
playing tokens
dice and shaker

Aim of the Game: To reach FINISH first

Number of Players: Any number

How to Play:

1. Shuffle card pack and lay out face up in a large
    rectangle. Decide which end of the bottom row has
    the START card, and find which end of the top row
    has the FINISH card by moving back and forth up the
    rows.
2. Decide who will go first.
3. As players roll the dice they move their tokens
    according to the number shown on the dice. If token
    lands on a black card, player moves his/her token
    FORWARDS that number of spaces. If the token lands
    on a red card, player moves the token BACKWARDS.
    (Thus any black card represents a ladder and any red
    card represents a snake.)
4. If the Jack, Queen or King are landed on, token
    moves forwards or backwards (depending on colour)
    five cards.
5. The player whose token reaches FINISH first is the
    winner.

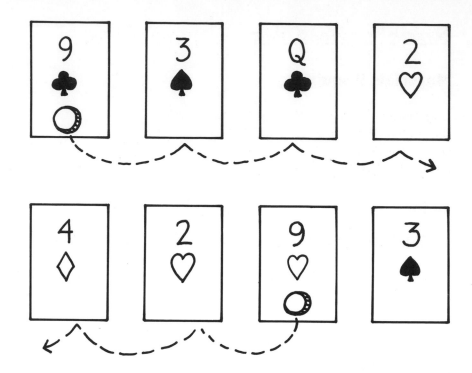

Match the Suit: Game One

Materials Required:

one pack of cards, with Jokers removed
piece of cardboard, approximately 20 cm x 20 cm
playing tokens
paper and pencils (for scoring)

Before You Start:

1. Make a Grid of Squares on card, as shown on page 28.

Aim of the Game: To score the highest number of
                    points

Number of Players: Any number

How to Play:

1. Shuffle card pack and place face down on the area marked A on the Grid of Squares.
2. Players place their tokens on any of the four squares of the Grid. Any number of players may rest their tokens on the same square.
3. Players take turns to turn over top card of pack, leaving it upturned on area B.
4. Players with tokens on squares of the same suit shown score the number shown on the upturned card. For example:

   If upturned card is a JACK and token is on the square of the same suit, score 15

If upturned card is a QUEEN and token is on the square of the same suit, score 20
If upturned card is a KING and token is on the square of the same suit, score 25

5. Once scores have been recorded, players move their tokens to another square or leave them where they are if they wish.
6. The next card is now turned over and game continues.
7. When all the cards have been upturned, game is over and scores are totalled. The player with the highest score is the winner.

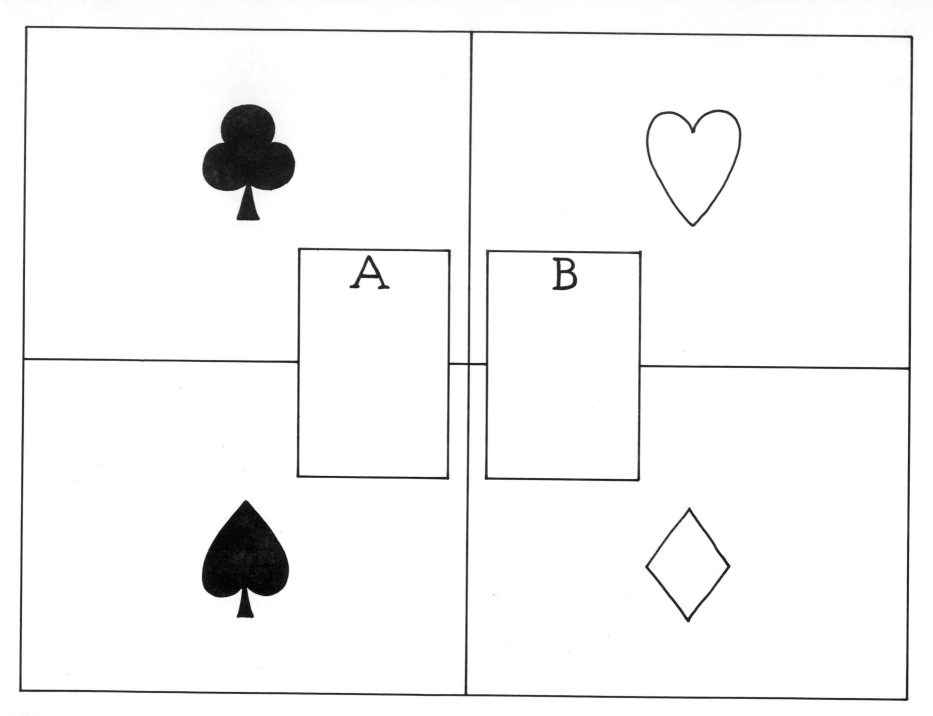

Match the Suit: Game Two

Materials Required:

one pack of cards, with one Joker removed
piece of cardboard, approximately 20 cm x 20 cm
playing tokens
paper and pencils (for scoring)

Before You Start:

I. Make Grid of Squares on card, as shown on page 28.

Aim of the Game: To score the lowest number of points

Number of Players: Any number

How to Play:

I. Shuffle card pack and place face down on the area marked A on the Grid of Squares.
2. Players place their tokens on any of the four squares. Any number of tokens may rest on the same square.
3. Players take turns to turn over top card of pack, leaving it upturned on area B.
4. Players with tokens on squares of the same suit as the upturned card score as follows:

        CARDS I TO 10 5
        JACK 10
        QUEEN 15
        KING 20

5. Once scores have been recorded, players move their tokens to another square or leave them where they are if they wish.
6. The next card is now turned over and game continues.
7. As soon as the Joker is turned up, game is over. Players total their scores and the lowest scoring player is the winner.

Spell a Word

Materials Required:

one pack of cards
playing tokens
dice and shaker
paper and pencils (for scoring)

Before You Start:

1. Supply players with paper and pencils for recording letters.
2. Place the Key where players can refer to it easily. (You may copy it onto a separate piece of paper if you wish.)

Key

If token lands on a:	Write down these letters:		
Joker	any vowel you need or would like		
King	a	e	
Queen	i	o	
Jack	u		
10	b	l	
9	k	y	
8	f	j	
7	q	w	
6	s	c	
5	y	p	
4	h	v	
3	d	n	
2	r	t	
1	m	g	z

Aim of the Game: To be the first player to make a word of four or more letters

Number of Players: Any number

How to Play:

1. Shuffle card pack and lay out face up in a circle.
2. Decide who will go first.
3. Players place playing tokens on any card they wish.
4. Players roll dice and move tokens around circle in a clockwise direction. When token lands on a card, player refers to Key and writes down the appropriate letters on his/her paper.
5. The first player to make a word of four or more letters is the winner and game is over. (Words must be in the dictionary!)

Variation:

1. Players agree on a long word, e.g. extravaganza, and write it on their papers. Players then cross off each letter that appears in the chosen word, noting that if a letter is repeated it can be ticked once only per turn.
2. The first player to cross off all the letters in the word is the winner.

Party Games

Think

Materials Required:

one pack of cards, with Jokers removed
wrapped sweets
playing tokens
thin cardboard
scissors
felt-tipped or ballpoint pen

Before You Start:

1. From the pack of cards take out the Royal Face cards and the 8s, 9s and 10s of all four suits. This is the Suit Pack. The remaining cards make up the 28 Card Pack. Keep the two packs separate until time for play.
2. Cut cardboard into sixteen 7 cm x 4 cm rectangles for the Subject Card Pack. In pen, write a subject on each card as follows:

planets	countries
capital cities	animals
colours	boys' names
girls' names	famous people
flowers	fruit
vegetables	ball games
sports	inventions
transport	machines

If you wish to include more subjects, make extra cards. You now have three packs of cards.

Aim of the Game: To earn sweets

Number of Players: Any number

How to Play:

1. Shuffle the Suit Pack and place face down.
2. Shuffle the 28 Card Pack and lay out face up in a circle. Decide which card is START.
3. Decide who will go first.
4. The player whose turn it is lifts the top card of the Suit Pack. If the card is a Heart, player moves his/her token in a clockwise direction to the next card in the circle showing Hearts — let's say this is the **5 of Hearts.** Player now lifts the top card of the Subject Cards Pack — let's say it reads **birds.** Therefore player must name 5 birds to earn a sweet. Both cards are replaced at the bottom of the packs and player's turn is over.
5. The game is over when all the sweets are gone.

Question/Answer

Materials Required:

one pack of cards, with Jokers removed
thin cardboard
scissors
felt-tipped or ballpoint pen
timer
wrapped sweets
paper and pencils (for scoring)
playing tokens
dice and shaker

Before You Start:

1. To make Question/Answer Card Pack, cut cardboard into 7 cm x 4 cm rectangles. On each one write a general knowledge question and answer. Make as many cards as possible. Here are some suggestions:

Q   What is the capital of Great Britain?
A   London
Q   How many moons does the planet Mars have?
A   Two
Q   How many are there in a baker's dozen?
A   Thirteen
Q   Where is the ulna bone in your body?
A   In your arm
Q   How do you spell Antarctica?
A   (Player must spell the word correctly.)
Q   What animal is measured in 'hands'?
A   Horse
Q   What author wrote the book *Matilda*?
A   Roald Dahl
Q   Who invented the ballpoint pen?
A   Biro

Q   What nationality was Amundsen, the first man to reach the South Pole?
A   Norwegian
Q   What is a guppy?
A   A fish
Q   In which country is the Mississippi River?
A   The United States of America

2. Supply players with paper and pencils for scoring.

Aim of the Game: To earn sweets

Number of Players: Any number

How to Play:

1. Shuffle card pack and lay out face up in a circle. Decide which card is START. Players place their tokens on this card and move them in a clockwise direction.
2. Shuffle Question/Answer Card Pack and place face down.
3. Decide who will go first.
4. Set timer for 10-15 minutes, depending on how long you would like the game to last.
5. Each player rolls the dice and moves his/her token around the circle according to the number shown. Players score the number of points shown on the card their tokens have landed on. For Royal Face cards, play is as follows:

If token lands on a JACK, the player opposite lifts top card of Question/Answer Card Pack and asks the question. If answer is correct, the player whose turn it is wins a sweet. If answer is incorrect, turn is over.

If token lands on a QUEEN, the player whose turn it is wins a sweet and turn is over.

If token lands on a KING, player scores 20 points and turn is over.

Question/Answer cards are not returned to the pack.

6. When timer rings, game is over and scores are totalled.
7. The player with the highest score is the winner. This player keeps the rest of the sweets as his/her prize.

Note: If the game does not last for 15 minutes, make more Question/Answer Cards.

Run Hop Skip Jump

Materials Required:

one pack of cards
scoreboard (in full view of players)

Before You Start:

1. Appoint someone to keep score, cut the deck, call the suit, and call the winners.

Aim of the Game: To earn points

Number of Players: Any number of teams with an equal number of players in each

How to Play:

1. Teams stand in straight lines and players are numbered 1, 2, 3, etc. (according to number of players in team). The 1s in one team compete against the 1s in the opposing team, the 2s against the 2s, and so on.
2. The deck of cards is shuffled, cut, and the suit called. Caller must include team members' numbers, e.g. 'Three! Club! Hop!' Team members take turns from the first to the last.

    If:
    a HEART is called, the team member RUNS
    a CLUB is called, the team member HOPS
    a DIAMOND is called, the team member SKIPS
      (could use a jump rope)
    a SPADE is called, the team member JUMPS
      (two feet together)

3. The players follow the instructions of the caller, moving around their teams and back to their places where they sit down. The first player to return to his/her place scores 10 points for that team.
4. The winning team is the one with the most points after all team members have had a turn.

Spell

Materials Required:

one pack of cards
felt-tipped or ballpoint pen
writing paper (for Spelling List)
thin card
scissors
playing tokens
wrapped sweets

Before You Start:

1. Make a Spelling List by writing down forty words (four columns of ten words each). Here are some suggestions:

table	picnic	rainbow	obedient
seven	orange	exactly	sandwich
grass	rubber	rubbish	precious
house	mother	cracked	eventful
fence	rabbit	failure	knitting
place	button	helpful	carriage
grand	school	ironing	slippery
visit	feeble	lasting	valuable
stick	dragon	opening	hundreds
berry	number	pasture	teaching

2. Cut card into 7 cm x 4 cm rectangles to form Spelling Words Pack. On each card write one word from the Spelling List.

Aim of the Game: To earn sweets

Number of Players: Any number

How to Play:

1. Shuffle Spelling Words Pack and place face down.
2. Shuffle card pack and lay out face up in a circle. Decide which card is START. Players place their tokens on this card.
3. Decide who will go first.
4. Players move their tokens around the circle according to the number of letters in their first name (e.g. Heather has seven letters, therefore player moves token seven cards each turn).
5. Tokens will land on either a red card or a black card. Players whose tokens land on a red card earn a sweet. If token lands on a black card, the player OPPOSITE lifts the top card of the Spelling Words Pack and reads the word. The player whose turn it is must spell the word correctly to earn a sweet. Turn is then over.
6. The game is over when the sweets run out, or when the Spelling Words Pack has been used up.

Games for One

Copy

Materials Required:

Royal Face cards from two packs of cards

Aim of the Game: To copy exactly the 'pattern' (this activity is just for fun)

Number of Players: One

How to Play:

1. Arrange twelve Royal Face cards from one of the packs, face up, in any pattern you like — rectangle, circle, or triangle.
2. Taking the Royal Face cards from the second pack, copy the first pattern, paying particular attention to the suits so that the Jack, Queen and King of each suit are placed in exactly the same way.

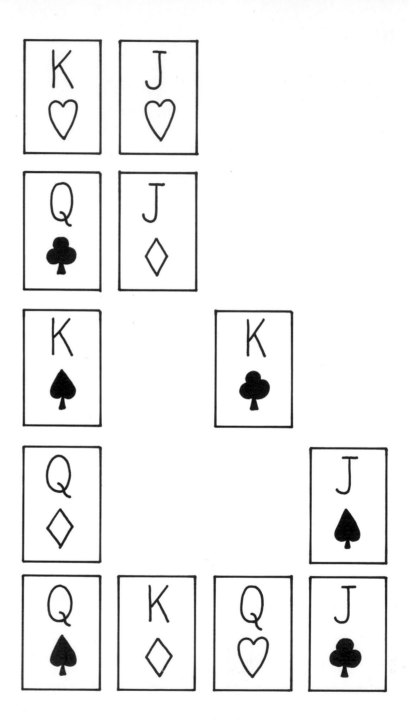

Solitary Sums

Materials Required:

one pack of cards, with Royal Face cards and Jokers
  removed
paper and pencils or calculator·(optional)

Aim of the Game: To have fun

Number of Players: One

How to Play:

I. Shuffle the card pack and lay out face down in a line.
Arrange some cards widthwise and some lengthwise,
as shown:

2. Decide which end is START and which is FINISH.
3. Beginning at START, turn over the cards that lie
lengthwise, one at a time, adding up their numbers in
your head as you go. Check your total with paper and
pencil or calculator if you wish.
4. Turn the cards face down again and repeat the game
with the cards that lie widthwise.

Variation:

Time yourself from start to finish with a clock or watch.
Record the time. Now repeat and try to beat your
previous time.

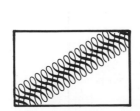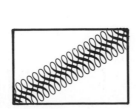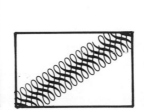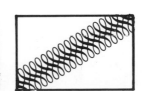